D0661248

CHRISTMAS MOVIE MOMENTS

Publications International, Ltd.

Cover and interior art: Shutterstock.com

Writer: Caroline Delbert

Contributing writers: Lisa Brooks, Amanda Kellogg

Louis Weber, CEO
Publications International, Ltd.
8140 Lehigh Avenue
Morton Grove, IL 60053

ISBN: 978-1-68022-644-7

Manufactured in China.

8 7 6 5 4 3 2 1

CONTENTS

A Charlie Brown Christmas................................... 4

White Christmas................................... 11

A Christmas Story................................... 15

Scrooged................................... 22

How the Grinch Stole Christmas................................... 32

National Lampoon's Christmas Vacation................................... 40

Rudolph the Red-Nosed Reindeer................................... 48

The Holiday................................... 53

The Santa Clause................................... 60

The Santa Clause 2: Mrs. Clause................................... 67

The Santa Clause 3................................... 74

It's a Wonderful Life................................... 81

The Polar Express................................... 96

Frosty the Snowman................................... 107

Home Alone................................... 116

Prancer................................... 132

Elf................................... 141

Die Hard................................... 153

Gremlins................................... 167

A Miracle on 34th Street................................... 176

A CHARLIE BROWN CHRISTMAS

First aired in 1965, *A Charlie Brown Christmas* led to dozens more *Peanuts* television specials. Nine-year-old Peter Robbins voiced the unlucky main character in this and several other specials during the 1960s. The cast of child actors was not credited in the original broadcast.

The original broadcast was sponsored by Coca-Cola and preempted an episode of *The Munsters*. Snoopy is the most durable breakout star of the Peanuts canon, but Lucy carved out her faux-grown-up niche in *A Charlie Brown Christmas*, including her iconic "Psychiatric Help 5¢" booth. She asks Charlie Brown if he has pantophobia, the fear of everything. He immediately says yes.

While Lucy has always wanted real estate for Christmas, Sally simply wants money.

First-time director Bill Melendez was not disheartened by his title character's woes as the director of the Christmas pageant—Melendez directed dozens of *Peanuts* titles over the next four decades and voiced Snoopy and Woodstock.

When Linus catches a snowflake on his tongue, he says it needs sugar.

In the special, Lucy suggests an *au courant* aluminum Christmas tree. When the gang feels guilty for mocking Charlie Brown's sympathetic little evergreen, they borrow ornaments from Snoopy's doghouse to decorate it.

During his iconic speech about the biblical Christmas story—quoting from the Gospel of Luke—Linus is not holding his beloved blanket. Later, at the end of the special, he uses it to prop up the tiny tree.

Although Lucy asks Schroeder to play "Jingle Bells" on his piano, the gang gathers to sing "Hark! The Herald Angels Sing" at the end of the special.

Snoopy's dancing became the stuff of inspirational-poster legend, but in this special he plays the guitar while the children dance on stage.

 8

In one of the only timely references in the special, Lucy tells Schroeder that anyone as allegedly great as Beethoven would have appeared on a bubble-gum card. Trading cards bundled with gum, candy, or even cigarettes were mostly phased out in favor of standalone packs of collectible cards.

Peppermint Patty does not appear in *A Charlie Brown Christmas*. Maybe the creators were reluctant to change her signature sandals for winter boots.

Rudolph the Red-Nosed Reindeer premiered one year before *A Charlie Brown Christmas.* The two, respectively, are the longest- and second-longest-running Christmas specials on U.S. network television.

WHITE CHRISTMAS

Released in 1954, *White Christmas* was actually the third film where star Bing Crosby sang the title song—the first two were *Holiday Inn* and *Blue Skies*. "White Christmas" was written by Irving Berlin, who also wrote "God Bless America."

Many Christmas movies have serious undertones, but most also revolve around something mystical—magic, time travel, visiting spirits. *White Christmas* opens in a town destroyed by war and follows two combat veterans as they put a show together.

Bing Crosby's character Bob appears on the fictional *Ed Harrison Show* to ask his army buddies to come to Vermont. He and Phil, played by Danny Kaye, stay at a lodge owned by their old commanding officer.

There's almost no snow in *White Christmas*, thwarting the main characters' plans at the ski lodge. It finally snows at the very, very end of the movie, when the backdrop of the Christmas show is raised to reveal falling snow.

Rosemary Clooney, aunt of George Clooney and popular 1950s recording artist, played costar Vera-Ellen's older sister. In reality, she was seven years younger.

While "White Christmas" was not eligible for an Oscar, Irving Berlin's song "Count Your Blessings (Instead of Sheep)" was nominated.

Phil sings that the best things happen when you're dancing. In fact, the song proves its own point: *White Christmas* was the top-grossing film of 1954.

A CHRISTMAS STORY

Released in 1983, *A Christmas Story* tapped into the nostalgic zeitgeist of the '80s using the almost-true stories of writer and narrator Jean Shepherd. The movie later inspired the television series *The Wonder Years*. In 2012, *A Christmas Story* was adapted into a Broadway musical.

Ralphie Parker was played by 12-year-old Peter Billingsley, who'd already accumulated ten years of acting credits. *Stand By Me* star Wil Wheaton also auditioned for the role.

The plot of *A Christmas Story* hinges on Ralphie's Christmas wish for a Red Ryder BB gun, which he mentions 28 times in the 93-minute movie. Viewers who endure all 24 hours of the yearly *A Christmas Story* marathon will hear Ralphie's wish more than 330 times.

Although he pines for a BB gun, Ralphie reluctantly asks Santa Claus for a football and receives a pink bunny suit from his Aunt Clara. His school theme about his Christmas wish receives a C+.

Ralphie's "old man," played by Darren McGavin, receives a lamp shaped like a leg and insists, to his wife's chagrin, that it is a "major award" instead of a contest prize. The film's director, Bob Clark, appears as a neighbor who marvels at the glowing leg lamp.

Younger brother Randy is stranded on his back in the snow because of his puffy snowsuit. Years later, baby Maggie Simpson suffers a similar fate in her star-shaped snowsuit.

The Parker family home is in Hammond, Indiana, a small Chicagoland city that was writer Jean Shepherd's real hometown. (Industrial Hammond actually had a larger population in 1960 than it did when the film was made.) But *A Christmas Story* was filmed in Cleveland and Toronto. A fan later bought the Cleveland house used for exterior shots of the Parker home and renovated it into a museum.

Jean Shepherd has a cameo as an irritated man
waiting in line to see Santa Claus.

Peter Billingsley's long acting resume came
in handy for the scene where Ralphie snaps
and beats up neighborhood bully Scut Farkus.
Although the dialogue sounds random and
nonsensical, it was scripted word for word.

The Parker family has Christmas dinner at a Chinese restaurant after their neighbor's dogs eat their turkey.

Ralphie's slow-motion swear word causes his mother to wash his mouth out with Palmolive soap (it has "a nice, piquant, after-dinner flavor"). But the film's most uncomfortable moment may be when Ralphie's friend Flick sticks his tongue to the frozen flagpole on a "triple dog dare."

SCROOGED

This loose adaptation of Charles Dickens's *A Christmas Carol* was released in 1988. Patrick Stewart, Kelsey Grammer, and James Earl Jones are just a few of the many stars who've played Ebenezer Scrooge during the film era.

Director Richard Donner may be best known for *Lethal Weapon* and 1978's *Superman* starring Christopher Reeve, but he also directed cult classics *The Omen* and *The Goonies*. Of course, he also shares his name with one of Santa's reindeer.

Bill Murray stars as "IBC" executive Frank Cross, and all three of Murray's real-life brothers appear in the movie. John Murray plays Frank's brother James.

Frank hallucinates while eating lunch in a restaurant and sees an eyeball in his water glass.

Scrooged replaces Bob Cratchit with Frank's assistant Grace Cooley. In place of Tiny Tim is Grace's son Calvin, who remains mute in the five years since his father died.

When a stagehand finds it difficult to attach tiny antlers to a mouse's head, Frank suggests the stagehand use staples. Many years later on *Gilmore Girls*, Melissa McCarthy's character Sookie makes a similar dark joke about replacing a spider's leg with a staple.

The Ghost of Christmas Past takes Frank back to 1955, where all child Frank wants for Christmas is a train set.

Young Frank plays the role of a dog named Frisbee on a children's show. Frisbee is a registered trademark of the Wham-O Corporation.

Karen Allen plays Frank's ex-girlfriend and one true love, Claire. Frank revisits their life together with the Ghost of Christmas Past. Claire and Frank meet on the sidewalk and begin dating. One of the movie's themes is Frank's terrible instincts for gift-giving—he gives Claire a set of Ginsu knives during their relationship.

Claire's nickname for Frank is "Lumpy."

The Ghost of Christmas Present is played by *Taxi* and *Unbreakable Kimmy Schmidt* star Carol Kane. While portraying the sprightly and somewhat violent character, Kane grabbed Bill Murray's lip so hard that his lip took several days to heal before filming could resume.

Frank's brother James, who stands in for Ebenezer Scrooge's nephew Fred, is shown playing Trivial Pursuit with his friends. Symbolism aside, 1988 was a big year for the board game: Its makers won a high-profile lawsuit in 1987 and sold rights to the game to Parker Brothers in 1988.

Claire works at a homeless shelter. When Frank stops by, a client named Herman mistakes him for Richard Burton. Frank refuses to buy Herman a cup of coffee. Burton is said to have quipped, "A man that hoards up riches and enjoys them not is like [a donkey] that carries gold and eats thistles."

Frank's holiday-stealing project is a live production of *A Christmas Carol*. Olympic gold-medal winner Mary Lou Retton, who is 4'9", appears as herself cast as Tiny Tim. Comedian Buddy Hackett and *M*A*S*H* star Jamie Farr are also in the fictional cast.

The Ghost of Christmas Future takes Frank to his own cremation, which only James and his wife Wendie attend. Fortunately, in the present, Grace replaces Frank's planned gift—a bath towel—with a VCR.

Longtime David Letterman bandleader Paul Shaffer appears in the film as a street musician. (So does Miles Davis!) In 2015, Shaffer and Bill Murray reunited for Murray's Netflix special *A Very Murray Christmas*.

Singer Robert Goulet good-naturedly appears in an IBC commercial for *Bob Goulet's Old-Fashioned Cajun Christmas*, part of Frank's "marketing by terror" campaign. Goulet uses a gondola pole to steer a canoe through an alligator-infested swamp.

HOW THE GRINCH STOLE CHRISTMAS

First aired in 1966, Dr. Seuss' *How the Grinch Stole Christmas*! was part of the wave of Christmas specials that included *A Charlie Brown Christmas* a year earlier. This animated adaptation of Dr. Seuss's 1957 children's book follows a similar story of holiday misguidance and redemption of the true meaning of Christmas.

The black-and-white Grinch character becomes green in the cartoon.

Director Chuck Jones was instrumental in persuading Dr. Seuss to adapt his book. Jones had worked with Dr. Seuss before and, more importantly, was established animation royalty. He won three Oscars during his seven-decade career and created countless characters, including the Coyote and Road Runner.
Meep meep!

Golden Age horror icon Boris Karloff narrates and voices the Grinch. The iconic "You're a Mean One, Mr. Grinch" was sung by Thurl Ravenscroft, known for his work on Disney animated musicals and as the voice of Tony the Tiger.

The Grinch and his dog Max, in their home on Mount Crumpit, have been putting up with Christmas in Whoville for 53 years.

The Grinch hates Christmas "most likely" because his heart is two sizes too small.

In his reverse-Santa act, the Grinch steals the stockings first. He raids the icebox and takes the Who pudding, roast beast, and other seasonal favorites. When Cindy Lou Who finds him taking their Christmas tree, he tells her one of the lights is broken. Finally, he steals the log for the fire.

Cindy Lou Who is voiced by June Foray, best known as the voice of Rocky the Flying Squirrel.

Dr. Seuss wrote the lyrics for the songs in the special. The song "Fahoo Fores" was written to sound like classical Latin, and some viewers actually requested translations. (A Latin translation of Dr. Seuss's book was released in 1998.) "You're a Mean One, Mr. Grinch" includes dozens of creative insults like *Your soul is an appalling dump heap* and *You have termites in your smile.*

When the Grinch sees the citizens of Whoville gather to sing on Christmas morning, he realizes that the Christmas trappings he stole—the things that helped irritate him for 53 years—are all beside the point.

Sharing Christmas with the Whos, the Grinch's heart grows three sizes. If it started out two sizes too small, that means it's now one size too large.

NATIONAL LAMPOON'S CHRISTMAS VACATION

Released in 1989, the third *Vacation* film earned the highest box office of the three to date. Chevy Chase, Beverly D'Angelo, and Randy Quaid returned along with a freshly recast set of Griswold children. The movie had a quite high $27 million budget.

John Hughes wrote the script of *National Lampoon's Christmas Vacation* as he had for the first two Vacation films. Hughes eventually wrote three more Christmas movies: *Home Alone*, *Home Alone 2*, and the remake of *Miracle on 34th Street*.

The Griswolds live in Chicago and Clark wears a Bears cap throughout the film.

Clark Griswold hangs 25,000 Christmas lights on his home.

Julia Louis-Dreyfus plays snotty next-door neighbor Margo Chester. Though she's known for her self-deprecating and good-natured physical humor, Louis-Dreyfus is also heiress to an energy fortune.

One of the movie's executive producers is pictured on the cover of *Clark's People* magazine.

Clark anxiously awaits his yearly bonus, which he plans to use for a swimming pool. (He daydreams about the future pool to the tune of Bing Crosby's version of tropical Christmas favorite "Mele Kalikimaka.") When an envelope finally arrives, it holds only a gift membership to the "Jelly of the Month" club.

Big Bang Theory and *Roseanne* star Johnny Galecki, in a very early role, appears as Rusty. He was also in the year's only other Christmas-themed movie, *Prancer*.

Randy Quaid's character Cousin Eddie hears Clark's why-I-oughta comments about his cheap boss and takes Clark literally, kidnapping the boss and bringing him to Clark. In a true Christmas miracle, hostage boss Frank Shirley —played by Brian Doyle-Murray—decides to reinstate the bonuses.

Everybody Loves Raymond star Doris Roberts plays Ellen's mother. By 1989, she had been acting in TV and movie roles for nearly 40 years. Her career continued apace until her death in 2016 at age 90.

Mae Questel, best known as the voice behind Betty Boop and Olive Oyl, plays dotty Aunt Bethany, who wraps a cat and a Jell-O mold as Christmas "gifts" and recites the Pledge of Allegiance as the Christmas Eve grace.

Clark's sled covered in "non-caloric silicon-based kitchen lubricant" rockets out of control and eventually comes to rest in a Wal-Mart parking lot. At the time, most of the east and west coast didn't have Wal-Marts. Even so, by 1990, Wal-Mart had become the largest retailer in the United States.

This Christmas movie ends on Christmas Eve.

RUDOLPH THE RED-NOSED REINDEER

First aired in 1964, *Rudolph the Red-Nosed Reindeer* is the longest-running Christmas special in the world. Rankin/Bass Productions went on to create many additional Christmas specials using both stop-motion and traditional animation. The company also made the animated classics *The Hobbit*, *The Last Unicorn*, and *ThunderCats*.

Rudolph the Red-Nosed Reindeer was created by Montgomery Ward copywriter Robert L. May and, years later, set to music by May's brother-in-law Johnny Marks. Incidentally, May was Jewish when he wrote the original poem but Catholic by the time the song came out—he converted in order to marry his second wife.

Sam the Snowman welcomes viewers to Christmastown in the North Pole. Burl Ives plays Sam the Snowman and narrates the film. He also sings the iconic title song.

When we first see Santa in the film, Mrs. Claus is chastising him: "Who ever heard of a skinny Santa!" That idea forms the basis of an Ally McBeal plot where *Parks & Recreation* star Jim O'Heir plays a department-store Santa fired in favor of a new "fit" Santa.

Santa's reindeer Donner is Rudolph's father and teaches young Rudolph about life in the North Pole, including the abominable snow monster ("Bumble") of the North. Later, Rudolph's red nose attracts the monster.

At the reindeer games, Rudolph meets a young doe named Clarice, who says she thinks Rudolph and his red nose are cute.

Hermey the elf wants to be a dentist and he and Rudolph decide to be "independent" and explore the world. They meet Yukon Cornelius and travel as a trio until Rudolph's red nose endangers the group by attracting the Bumble. Rudolph leaves in order to protect his friends.

The Island of Misfit Toys is supervised by a winged lion named King Moonracer. Later, Santa promises Rudolph that he'll find homes for all the misfit toys.

When Rudolph is born, Santa says he doesn't think Rudolph and his red nose will ever be able to help pull the sleigh. But when fog threatens the Christmas deliveries, Santa makes a climactic decision to let Rudolph save the day. The elves celebrate by singing "A Holly Jolly Christmas," which Johnny Marks wrote for the special. Burl Ives's enduring single of the song has charted off and on since its release in 1965.

THE HOLIDAY

Released in 2006, *The Holiday* is Nancy Meyers's only Christmas movie to date—a surprise given her penchant for heartwarming comedy with almost fairy-tale flourishes. Kate Winslet and Cameron Diaz anchor the extensive A-list cast.

Winslet as Iris and Diaz as Amanda decide to exchange homes using a proto-AirBnB service. The interiors were all constructed on a set.

Meyers's film oeuvre is filled with people who become wealthy by working as bakers, playwrights, and wedding-dress designers, for example. In *The Holiday*, Iris is a society columnist and Amanda is a movie-trailer producer. Their love interests are a composer and a book editor.

Amanda asks Iris if there are any men in her quiet Surrey, England town and Iris says "zero."

Dustin Hoffman has a cameo in the movie—he happened to be driving by the filming location and was added to a scene on the spot.

In Los Angeles, Iris meets Amanda's elderly neighbor Arthur when he can't remember his address and needs a ride home. Arthur calls this a "meet cute," the entertainment-industry term for a first meeting that is novel and amusing. In an episode of *Sex and the City*, Carrie Bradshaw parodies the idea when she shelters beneath an awning during a downpour and finds a handsome man there. As she describes the idea of the meet cute, he grows nervous and afraid and runs back into the downpour.

Jude Law plays Iris's brother Graham, who meets Amanda the first night she stays in Iris's cottage. Amanda overhears Graham talking to "Sophie" and "Olivia" and grows jealous before finding out they are Graham's young daughters. Olivia says Amanda looks like her Barbie doll.

After Amanda reveals that she hasn't cried since she was 15, Graham says he cries at everything: "A good book, a great film, a birthday card, I weep." Amanda does eventually cry in the taxi to the airport. When she returns to Iris's cottage to profess her love, Graham is also crying.

Jack Black plays Iris's eventual love interest Miles, a composer, who is touched by her attention to Arthur and writes a theme song for him.

Arthur is a retired screenwriter with an upcoming "lifetime achievement" event. He's nervous and hesitant because he can't climb stairs without using a walker. Iris helps him exercise to get ready for the ceremony. She also throws him a Hanukkah party.

Amanda is shown working on a movie trailer for a fictional project starring James Franco and Lindsay Lohan.

THE SANTA CLAUSE

Released in 1994, the original *The Santa Clause* coincided with star Tim Allen's peak ratings on TV's *Home Improvement*. Walt Disney Pictures was in the midst of a live-action golden age of sorts, albeit dwarfed by the mammoth success of its animated features.

The Santa Clause was directed by John Pasquin, who worked with Allen on *Home Improvement*. Pasquin has only directed four films, three of which star Allen.

The movie's premise doesn't sound very Disney at first: Advertising executive Scott Calvin accidentally kills Santa Claus and, as a result, must replace him. The titular clause is a piece of paperwork that Scott finds in Santa's pocket. When Scott puts on Santa's suit, he becomes Santa Claus.

*At the North Pole, lead elf
Bernard tells Scott and his son
Charlie that Scott must return to
the North Pole by Thanksgiving
the following year.*

Judy the Elf has spent 1,200 years perfecting her hot cocoa recipe: Not too hot, extra chocolate, shaken not stirred.

Scott receives a surprising delivery of many packages, which turns out to be the "naughty or nice" list. Charlie has been a Santa Claus skeptic but he embraces his dad's new role. Unfortunately, Scott's ex-wife and her new husband think Scott has lost his mind—in eleven months his hair has turned white, he has grown a huge beard that can't be removed, and he's gained a lot of weight. Scott initially claims he gained weight because he was stung by a bee.

On Christmas Eve, the police find Scott in his Santa livery and arrest him. What's worse, at the good little girl's house he inadvertently drinks soy milk.

Scott's ex-wife and her husband are finally convinced when Scott brings them the gifts they longed for but did not receive as children. One is an Oscar Mayer weiner whistle.

Bernard the elf gives Charlie a snow globe so he can see his dad anytime he wants.

The Santa Clause made nearly $190 million on a budget of $22 million.

THE SANTA CLAUSE 2: THE MRS. CLAUSE

Released in 2002, *The Santa Clause 2: The Mrs. Clause* was director Michael Lembeck's first feature film after directing more than 250 episodes of television. Since he began directing in 1989, that's an average of 19 episodes a year.

The Keeper of the Handbook of Christmas, an elf named Curtis, tells Scott that he must have a wife in order to remain Santa Claus. Spencer Breslin, the star of Disney's *The Kid* opposite Bruce Willis, plays Curtis.

Scott plans to go home to find a wife, but he's even more motivated after finding out his son Charlie is on the naughty list. He meets Charlie's principal Carol and begins to fall for her.

Charlie now has a half-sister, Lucy, who loses a tooth at a climactic moment in the film.

Curtis creates a life-size toy Santa Claus to stand in for Scott at the North Pole. The toy Santa is programmed too strictly and declares that the whole world is on the naughty list. He creates a totalitarian regime complete with tin soldiers as enforcers. The tin-soldier costumes the actors wore were made of fiberglass and weighed over 50 pounds each.

Scott discusses his search for a Mrs. Claus at the Council of Legendary Figures meeting, which includes the Sandman, Father Time, and Cupid.

Carol and Scott go on a date to the school faculty Christmas party, transported by a magical sleigh ride.

When Scott tells Carol he is Santa Claus, she thinks he must be making fun of her. Charlie convinces her by showing her his magical snow globe.

Because of the nearing end-date of his Santa contract, Scott begins to revert to his pre-Santa looks and has much less magic.

After Bernard the elf is thrown in toy Santa's jail for dissension, Curtis comes to ask Scott to help overthrow toy Santa. Curtis's jetpack is broken, but Lucy has lost a tooth, and they convince the Tooth Fairy to fly them back to the North Pole.

Mother Nature, played by Aisha Tyler, performs Scott and Carol's wedding ceremony.

THE SANTA CLAUSE 3

Released in 2006 with a budget of just $12 million, *The Santa Clause 3* was not especially well received by critics, but it still made over $111 million at the box office. Its plot takes a turn for the *Star Trek* with time travel and alternate timelines—maybe having a *Lost* star in the cast, Elizabeth Mitchell as Carol, made an impression on the filmmakers.

Everybody Loves Raymond
**star Peter Boyle returns
as Father Time. This was
the final film to be released
before Boyle's death.**

Four years have passed since Scott and Carol were married and they are now expecting a baby.

Martin Short joins the mostly returning cast as villain Jack Frost. At a meeting of the Council of Legendary Figures, Mother Nature accuses Jack Frost of trying to upstage Santa Claus in order to push Jack Frost's own agenda. He is sentenced to community service at the North Pole—decorating.

Carol grows homesick for her family to such an extent that Scott plans for her parents to visit the North Pole. They believe Scott is a toymaker in Canada, and Scott and the North Pole crew must keep up the ruse.

The movie was filmed mostly in Canada, which means Canada is portraying the North Pole masquerading as Canada.

In this new timeline, Jack Frost turns the North Pole into a resort for tourists.

Jack Frost learns that there's an "escape clause" in the Santa contract, using a special snow globe from the North Pole that shows Scott as the latest in the long line of Santa Clauses. He tricks Scott and sends them both back in time to 1994, making himself the new Santa Claus and rewriting their future.

Without his appointment as Santa Claus, Scott lacks purpose and heart in his parallel life. He is overworked and ignores Charlie. He never remarries, and his ex-wife and her husband are now divorced as well.

Lucy figured out Jack Frost's plan and tried to prevent it—he froze her parents and locked her in a closet to stop her. Even so, it is Lucy who unfreezes Jack Frost with a warm hug.

Carol has a healthy baby boy and the couple names him Buddy. Is this in homage to *Elf's* main character? We can't be sure.

IT'S A WONDERFUL LIFE

Released in 1946, *It's a Wonderful Life* was a box-office disappointment, released on the heels of blockbuster postwar drama *The Best Years of Our Lives*.

Director Frank Capra and star Jimmy Stewart made a total of three movies together. Capra often called It's a Wonderful Life *his favorite of all his films.*

Donna Reed stars as Mary Bailey (nee Hatch), a decade before her long-running series *The Donna Reed Show*.

The movie is based on a short story by Philip Van Doren Stern, with shades of the "what if?" motif of *A Christmas Carol*.

Clarence is brought up to speed on the George Bailey life story, beginning when George saves his younger brother Harry from drowning and loses the hearing in one ear as a result.

The Bedford Falls pharmacist, Mr. Gower, learns his son has died of influenza and is so distraught that he nearly poisons one of his patrons by accident. George notices the mistake and prevents the additional tragedy.

George Bailey is despondent on Christmas Eve, ready to jump from a bridge, when his guardian angel Clarence is sent to save him.

Mary and George dance together in the school gym as the floor opens to reveal a pool. The scene was shot at the real "swim gym" at Beverly Hills High School in Los Angeles.

George and Mary walk home from the high school dance and sing the song to which they first danced together, "Buffalo Gals." The movie is set in a fictional New York town about two hours from Buffalo.

Circumstances cause George to take over the family's banking business with his uncle Billy, who keeps a pet raven at the bank. George gives up his dream of traveling the world.

On the night of their wedding, Mary and George are serenaded by a police officer and a cab driver. The pair are named Bert and Ernie. The Muppets's official position is that Bert and Ernie's names on *Sesame Street* are a mere coincidence.

George uses his college fund to send Harry to college instead and uses his honeymoon fund to help stave off a run on the bank after the stock market crashes.

The villain of *It's a Wonderful Life* is Mr. Potter, the evil, greedy banker who wants to drive Bailey Building and Loan out of business. He tries to buy out George Bailey's interest in the Building and Loan with a ludicrously lucrative job offer. Later, he finds that he's taken Uncle Billy's money—$8,000—by mistake, and keeps it to help drive the Building and Loan out of business.

Mr. Potter offers George $20,000 a year, at a time when the average salary was about $3,000 and a new car cost just $1,500.

In the scenario where George Bailey was never born, Bedford Falls has become Pottersville.

*Without George in
her life, Mary has
become a librarian.*

Harry has drowned in the alternate timeline. The men he saved in World War II have died without Harry to save them.

George isn't there to prevent the pharmacist from giving his customer poison. The pharmacist goes to prison for manslaughter.

Clarence sees the power of George's good nature and generosity all along, but only after seeing the grim alternative does George realize his own value. He races through the town and then home to his family.

In Heaven, Clarence was told that he would earn his wings if he saved George Bailey. At the end of the film, George and Mary's youngest daughter Zuzu says, "Every time a bell rings, an angel gets his wings."

Clarence leaves a note behind. "Dear George: Remember, no man is a failure who has friends!"

It's a Wonderful Life was nominated for five Academy Awards but didn't win any. The filmmakers did win a technical Academy Award—given at a different ceremony—for their invention of a new way to make faux snow (snaux?). They combined fire-extinguisher foam with soap flakes. This replaced what has been described as "corn flakes painted white" and eliminated the need to redub all the sound as actors crunched them underfoot. Falling snow is another story. In 2012, industry expert Roland Hathaway told the *New York Times*, "There are some pictures that we found from '50s movie sets, where people were actually just shoveling asbestos into a fan."

The people of Bedford Falls gather in the Bailey home during the final scene of the movie and sing "Auld Lang Syne." We think of this as a New Year's Eve song now, but its message is poignant for George Bailey: His pain and misfortune drove him to want to "forget" himself to the minds of his loved ones. Is it right to forget? George learns that it isn't.

THE POLAR
EXPRESS

Released in 2004, *The Polar Express* is an adaptation of Chris Van Allsburg's 1985 children's book. The movie set records at the time: its $165 million budget was the highest to date for an animated film, and it was the first full-length digital-capture film.

Van Allsburg's book won the Caldecott Medal (for "the most distinguished American picture book for children") in 1986.

Director Robert Zemeckis has embraced cutting-edge technology for his entire long career, including the *Back to the Future* movies and even the black-comedy effects in *Death Becomes Her*. He threw himself into full-motion-capture technology beginning with *The Polar Express*.

Zemeckis's longtime collaborator Alan Silvestri composed the music for *The Polar Express*—their tenth project together.

The Polar Express, bound for the North Pole, picks Hero Boy up at 11:55 p.m. at his house.

Tom Hanks appears as the Conductor, the Hobo, Santa Claus, and more. This was his third collaboration with Robert Zemeckis.

Only one character on the train is ever mentioned by name, Billy, who is also called Lonely Boy.

On the train, the children are served hot chocolate. This is pleasingly simple in the age of the Hogwarts Express.

The train is forced to stop by a caribou on the tracks.

Hero Boy and the Hobo use skis as they chase Hero Girl down the train's snowy roof.

The train encounters "the steepest downhill grade in the world," Glacier Gulch. In real life, the steepest train line in the world not pulled by a cable is the Mt. Pilatus railway line in Switzerland. The line runs for less than 3 miles and climbs over one mile in altitude using special cog wheels that run along a toothed track.

Aerosmith singer Steven Tyler makes a cameo appearance as an elf in a rock band at the North Pole.

Hero Boy is chosen to receive the first gift of Christmas: a silver sleigh bell that has come loose from the reindeer harness on Santa's sleigh.

When the Conductor punches Hero Boy's ticket, it says "Believe."

The conductor punches "Lead" into Hero Girl's ticket.

Hero Boy loses the sleigh bell through a hole in his pants pocket. He finds it again in a box under his Christmas tree at home.

Lonely Boy's address, 11344 Edbrooke, is on Chicago's far south side in the Roseland neighborhood—director Robert Zemeckis's real childhood home. The clock at the North Pole is modeled on the Pullman Factory Clock Tower in the neighboring Pullman community.

Author and illustrator Chris Van Allsburg modeled the Polar Express on a historical train he played on as a child. The engine was displayed in his hometown of Grand Rapids, Michigan.

Zemeckis's wife Leslie Zemeckis worked as a motion-capture model for the film. She did the same for *Beowulf* and *A Christmas Carol*.

*Hero Boy's sleigh bell
can be heard by all
who truly believe.*

Josh Groban sings the movie's theme song, "Believe."

Hero Boy's real name is never mentioned in the film or the original book.

FROSTY THE SNOWMAN

First aired in 1969, *Frosty the Snowman* adapted a popular Christmas song recorded by Gene Autry in 1950. Rankin/Bass Productions made Frosty as part of their long list of animated holiday specials.

Gene Autry had recorded "Rudolph the Red-Nosed Reindeer" as a single in 1949 after other artists turned it down. "Rudolph" was a hit, and this inspired songwriters Walter Rollins and Steve Nelson to write "Frosty" and send it to Autry.

The production designer of Frosty was artist Paul Coker. He worked on numerous Rankin/Bass specials in tandem with his work for Mad magazine. In fact, Coker, now in his late 80s, still makes new work for Mad.

The children's teacher hires a magician named Professor Hinkle to entertain the students. His act is unsuccessful but the rabbit from his hat shows him up. (As fellow failed musician Bullwinkle once said: "No doubt about it—I gotta get another hat.")

Emmy-winning comedian Jimmy Durante narrates the special and sings the titular song. By 1969, Durante had worked for nearly fifty years in vaudeville, radio, film, and television. Frosty introduced him to a new generation of viewers and is likely his most enduring work, though many also remember his song "Make Someone Happy" from its appearance in *Sleepless in Seattle*.

When the children build a snowman together, they consider many names for him, including Christopher Columbus, Oatmeal, and Harold.

The snowman's first words to the children are "Happy birthday!" In a sense, it's Frosty's own birthday, so he's not wrong. Odds are also higher than 1 in 20 that Frosty shares a birthday with one of those six children.

Frosty is brought to life by Professor Hinkle's magical hat, which he didn't realize is magical.

A traffic cop realizes he's been talking to a snowman who had come to life, and he swallows his police whistle.

Frosty must travel to the North Pole because it's a warm day and he's beginning to melt. The 2013 Disney hit *Frozen* takes a less pragmatic take when snowman Olaf sings a love song to summer. Of course, Olaf later receives a Truman Show-style personal snowcloud to enable his own "endless summer"—if only Frosty had been so lucky.

Karen is the one who names Frosty. She, Frosty, and Hocus Pocus the rabbit stow away on a train because they don't have any money. They nestle Frosty in the refrigerated car with the Christmas treats.

In a plot largely concerned with weather, the gang next realizes that Karen will freeze at the North Pole. They must ask Santa Claus for help. Some animals build a fire, but villain Professor Hinkle blows it out. They hide in a greenhouse and he locks them inside, where Frosty melts. When Santa arrives, the gust of cold wind revives Frosty.

Santa Claus sentences Professor Hinkle to write "I am very sorry for what I did to Frosty" a hundred zillion times before Santa will consider giving him a new magic hat.

Frosty returns each year with the Christmas snow.

*Although the plot of the
Frosty special revolves
around Christmas and the
North Pole, the original song
was simply about snow.*

HOME ALONE

Released in 1990, *Home Alone* brought together writer John Hughes and director Chris Columbus. The movie was an enormous hit, making over $500 million against its $18 million budget and reigning as the highest grossing live-action comedy for the next 21 years. It is the highest-grossing Christmas movie of all time, not even counting its numerous sequels.

Director Chris Columbus previously had a modest success with 1987's *Adventures in Babysitting*, which also featured a stranded minor who must save the day. (This is also the arc of the two Harry Potter films he directed and of *The Goonies*, which he wrote.)

John Williams composed the film's well known score. The swooping, orchestral sound with heavy use of Christmas-y bells resurfaces in director Chris Columbus's two Harry Potter films.

Kevin's siblings and cousins all stay in the house before the big trip, making a total of 11 children in one house.

Macaulay Culkin plays 8-year-old Kevin McCallister, whose family leaves for the airport and flies to Paris without him. He is stranded in their suburban Chicagoland home.

The photo of Buzz's "girlfriend" was of the art director's son made up to look like a girl, in order to avoid making fun of a girl portrayed in earnest.

Macaulay Culkin's younger brother Kieran Culkin, who went on to star in movies like *Igby Goes Down* and *Scott Pilgrim vs. the World*, appears in the movie as Fuller.

Kevin's favorite pizza topping is cheese. He orders his "very own cheese pizza" from Little Nero's. The driver knocks over the McCallisters's lawn ornament with his Plymouth Horizon, a car that was thankfully sunsetted in 1990.

The McCallister kids are afraid of their neighbor, Old Man Marley, who is rumored to have killed his family with a snow shovel. Kevin sees Old Man Marley at the drugstore and is so frightened that he accidentally shoplifts a toothbrush.

John Candy appears in the film as a polka player who helps Kevin's mom. He filmed his entire part in just one day.

In the confusion and conflict at the beginning of the film, Kevin wishes for his family to disappear. As a result, he's euphoric at first when he realizes that he's been left alone. But by the time he goes to see Santa, he asks for his family to come back.

Marv, played by *Wonder Years* narrator Daniel Stern, leaves the water running in all of the houses he and Harry rob so that he can call them the Wet Bandits.

At the store, Kevin buys milk, orange juice, and fabric softener—what every 8 year old needs.

Macaulay Culkin drew the map that Kevin uses to show where his traps are set up.

The role of Harry was first offered to Robert De Niro, who turned it down. De Niro went on to play memorable comic villains in *Stardust* and *Meet the Parents*.

In the scene where a tarantula crawls on Marv's face, Daniel Stern had to mime the scream because a real scream would have "scared" the spider. The sound was dubbed in afterward.

Joe Pesci went on to play Harry. He and Robert De Niro appeared together in another of 1990's critical favorites: *Goodfellas*.

In a method move, Joe Pesci avoided Macaulay Culkin on set in order to appear more "mean" and add realism to Culkin's performance.

Macaulay Culkin improved the line, "You guys give up? Or are you thirsty for more?"

In the scene where Marv sneaks in through the window, the ornaments he must step on were actually made of candy.

The black and white movie Kevin watches, *Angels with Filthy Souls*, is a parody of the 1938 James Cagney classic *Angels with Dirty Faces*. A similar parody appears in *Home Alone 2: Lost in New York*.

The fake snow used in the movie was later given to the Lyric Opera of Chicago and has appeared in numerous productions.

John Hughes wrote the part of Kevin with Macaulay Culkin in mind, but auditioned several hundred other boys just to be sure he made the right decision.

At the beginning of the movie, most of the shots of Macaulay Culkin are from above his head in order to make him appear smaller and weaker. By the end, most of the shots are from below him, and he appears stronger and more confident.

Marv is thwarted by a falling clothes iron, the tarantula on his face, tar and nails on the stairs, and a BB gun shot through the dog door.

Harry runs into glue and feathers, a blowtorch to the head, and a burning-hot doorknob.

Both burglars fall victim to toy cars on the floor and the swinging paint cans.

PRANCER

Released in 1989, *Prancer* is Sam Elliott's only Christmas movie role to date. The movie is modest by holiday standards, with a first-time writer and less than $20 million in box-office gross.

Sam Elliott plays John Riggs, a struggling farmer, whose daughter Jessica befriends a reindeer.

Jessica hears her father talking to her aunt, Sarah, and is upset to hear that they plan to send Jessica to live with Sarah.

Ariana Richards appears as Carol, whose fluffy bangs are very serious even by '80s standards. Richards is known for her role as Lex in *Jurassic Park*, but as an adult she is also an accomplished oil painter. She has even done work for Karolyn Grimes, the actress who played Zuzu in *It's a Wonderful Life*.

When Jessica and her friend Carol are walking home from school, a reindeer decoration from the town's sleigh display falls into the street. Jessica uses the order given in "The Night Before Christmas" to determine that it is Prancer.

Cloris Leachman, known for playing sneaky landlady Phyllis on *The Mary Tyler Moore Show*, plays the Riggs's reclusive neighbor Mrs. McFarland. Jessica angers Mrs. McFarland by sledding through her rose bushes.

Jessica finds Prancer in her father's barn and lures him out using Christmas cookies.

In order to buy oats for Prancer, Jessica must find some money—her family is barely getting by as it is. She apologizes to Mrs. McFarland and asks if she can do any paid work. Mrs. McFarland offers to pay Jessica for cleaning part of her house.

Jessica visits her local shopping mall Santa. She assures him she knows he isn't the real Santa Claus but hopes he can pass a message along to the real Santa because of his connections.

The mall Santa shares the touching story with a local newspaper editor, who writes about it and brings attention Jessica doesn't want. The title of the newspaper article about Prancer is "Yes, Santa, there are still Virginias." Later in the movie, Jessica asks her father to read to her from the original "Yes, Virginia, there is a Santa Claus."

John Riggs finds out about Prancer after the reindeer frees all the animals from the barn and wreaks havoc inside the Riggs home. Prancer also eats a pie.

Abe Vigoda appears in the film as Dr. Benton, a veterinarian reluctant to visit Jessica's alleged reindeer guest, a wild animal. She cajoles him by insisting that doctors never help anyone and hanging from the open window of his pickup truck. *Prancer* was one of several dozen roles Vigoda completed after he was mistakenly referred to as dead in a major magazine in 1982. In fact, Vigoda passed away in his sleep in 2016 at the ripe old age of 94.

Jessica's father sees Prancer's fame as a way to help the family out of their financial problems, and he agrees to sell Prancer to the local butcher. Although Jessica fears the worst, the butcher only uses Prancer as an attraction to help sell Christmas trees.

John Riggs finally comes around to Jessica's point of view. Together, they take Prancer to Antler Ridge, where John says Santa Claus will be sure to find him. They see a streak of light and find that Prancer has left hoofprints to the edge of a cliff—with no way out but to fly.

The reindeer "actor" who portrayed Prancer is named Boo.

ELF

Released in 2003, *Elf* found star Will Ferrell at the beginning of a huge wave of post-*Saturday Night Live* success. The movie made more than $220 million on its budget of $33 million. Although there have been a Broadway musical adaptation and a stop-motion TV special, *Elf* has no sequels to date.

Director Jon Favreau went in a new direction with his second film. The *Swingers* star's directorial debut was *Made,* a crime comedy starring his longtime friend and collaborator Vince Vaughn.

Will Ferrell stars as Buddy, an orphaned human infant who crawls into Santa's sack on Christmas Eve and ends up at the North Pole. There, he is raised by Papa Elf.

Bob Newhart plays Papa Elf. Newhart has honed his characteristic dry humor in a career lasting sixty years and counting. Elf is one of just a small handful of holiday roles.

Ed Asner appears as Santa Claus. He's best known for his role as Lou Grant in *The Mary Tyler Moore Show,* which is often cited alongside its contemporary *The Bob Newhart Show* as one of the best television shows in history. But younger viewers may recognize him as the voice of Carl in Pixar's hit *Up.*

The "Kringle 3000" is a 500-reindeer-power jet engine used to power Santa's sleigh.

Buddy believes he is an elf until he overhears two elves talking about him. He lacks toymaking ability and calls himself a "cotton headed ninny muggings."

Leon the Snowman, voiced by musician Leon Redbone, helps to convince Buddy that he should go to New York and seek out his birth father. But Santa tells Buddy that his birth father is on the naughty list because of his selfishness.

As Buddy is leaving the North Pole, his friends are startled by a well-wisher in the form of Mr. Narwhal. Jon Favreau provided the voice of Mr. Narwhal.

The design for Santa's workshop in Elf is based on the classic *Rudolph the Red-Nosed Reindeer*, and 2014's stop-motion Elf special is a pastiche of Rudolph and other animated classics.

*When Buddy finds his birth
father's office, his father
initially believes Buddy is a
singing telegram.*

James Caan plays Buddy's father Walter Hobbs. Caan is best known as Sonny Corleone from the *Godfather* films but has appeared in several children's and family films in his more recent career.

The elves try to stick to the "four main food groups": candy, candy canes, candy corn, and syrup. Buddy prepares a bag of spaghetti covered in maple syrup for Emily Hobbs to take to work.

Walter Hobbs works at a children's publisher. He is upset when Buddy mentions his birth mother, Susan Wells, and has Buddy removed by security. A guard sees Buddy's outfit and says Buddy should go back to Gimbels—the department store made famous by *Miracle on 34th Street*. Buddy takes the sarcasm literally and finds a job at Gimbels.

In real life, Gimbels closed in the 1980s.

Peter Dinklage appears in *Elf* as Miles Finch, a famous children's author whom Walter Hobbs wants to bring to his publishing company. Dinklage was relatively unknown when *Elf* was made, but his buzzy star turn in *The Station Agent* came just a month before *Elf's* release.

Miles Finch and Buddy fight after Buddy mistakes him for an elf. Years later, Dinklage played a similar role on *30 Rock*, where Tina Fey's Liz Lemon character repeatedly mistook him for a child.

At Gimbels, Buddy meets and likes Jovie, a low-energy fellow employee who says she's just trying to get through the holidays. Buddy's newly discovered half-brother, Michael, advises Buddy that he should ask Jovie on a date "to eat food."

On Christmas Eve, Santa crashes his sleigh in Central Park and breaks the Kringle 3000. He needs Buddy's help but he also needs Christmas spirit in order to fly again. Buddy's infectious enthusiasm has swayed Jovie, who leads the crowd in song. But the deal is only sealed when Buddy convinces stressed-out Walter to sing as well.

Will Ferrell turned down the idea of a sequel.

DIE HARD

Released in 1988, *Die Hard* is persistently named as one of the best action movies ever made and often one of the best movies period. It earned over $140 million against a budget of $28 million. Bruce Willis had starred in *Moonlighting* since 1985, but *Die Hard* made him an instant action star. There have been five *Die Hard* films to date.

The film was based on a novel by Roderick Thorp called *Nothing Lasts Forever*. Technically the novel is a sequel, and the original novel, *The Detective*, was adapted into a film starring Frank Sinatra as the "McClane" character.

Director John McTiernan was in the middle of a three-movie winning streak: 1987's *Predator*, *Die Hard*, and 1990's *The Hunt for Red October*. These are also the three best-reviewed films of his career.

The action in Die Hard *takes place during a Christmas party at fictional Nakatomi Plaza in Los Angeles.*

Bruce Willis stars as John McClane, a NYPD detective who travels to Los Angeles on Christmas Eve in order to spend Christmas with his children. Arnold Schwarzenegger, Richard Gere, and Mel Gibson were all considered for the role before it went to Bruce Willis.

McClane's wife Holly works at Nakatomi Plaza. A limousine driver named Argyle drives McClane from the airport to the party. While McClane is changing clothes, a group of terrorists arrive and take the rest of the party hostage.

Alan Rickman appears in his first movie role as terrorist leader Hans Gruber. He went on to play countless charismatic villains and antiheroes, most notably as Professor Severus Snape in the Harry Potter film series.

The terrorists, who are from Germany, say they plan to steal bearer bonds from the Nakatomi Corporation. Bearer bonds have no fixed owner and are almost impossible to recover after a theft. Their benefit of anonymity has also been their undoing, and new bearer bonds are issued only very rarely.

McClane first tries to get the attention of someone outside the building by pulling the fire alarm.

A henchman named Tony chases and attacks McClane. After McClane wins the fight, he uses Tony's radio to notify the LAPD.

Reginald VelJohnson appears as LAPD sergeant Al Powell. VelJohnson played many police officers during his career, including as sitcom dad Carl Winslow in *Family Matters*.

When Sergeant Powell gets the call to Nakatomi Plaza, he is buying Twinkies at the store. He is on desk duty, which he asked for after a terrible incident where he shot and killed a boy who had a toy gun.

At first, Sergeant Powell is misled by a terrorist who's pretending to be the receptionist at Nakatomi Plaza. McClane gets his attention by dropping the body of a terrorist onto Sergeant Powell's police car.

Argyle the limo driver has been trapped in the parking garage, and when he finally turns on the TV in his limo, he sees the hostage situation on the news.

McClane discovers and corners Hans Gruber, but Gruber pretends to be a hostage.

Holly McClane is estranged from her husband, and at the beginning of the movie they fight because she is using her maiden name. But later, when a terrorist begins smashing decorations, she knows it means McClane is still alive, and she's relieved and happy.

Hans Gruber mocks McClane by calling him "Mister Cowboy." McClane responds with his now-signature line: "Yippee-ki-yay, [expletive]."

Sergeant Powell is finally able to use his gun again when he sees a terrorist aiming an assault rifle at McClane.

The office building that "played" Nakatomi Plaza is Fox Plaza in Los Angeles.

Although the terrorists were German, only a couple of the actors who played them were German. Among the non-Germans is actor and ballet dancer Alexander Godunov. Bruce Willis was actually born in Germany.

Beethoven's Ninth Symphony, known for containing "Ode to Joy," features prominently throughout the movie.

At the moment when the terrorists begin shooting, McClane is testing advice he received on the plane: to relax after a long flight by taking off your shoes and feeling the carpet under your feet. When he removes the shoes of a terrorist he complains that they're "smaller than my sister's."

GREMLINS

Released in 1984, *Gremlins* is a violent, very dark comedy that begins with an exotic Christmas gift. Steven Spielberg produced the film and appeared in a brief cameo. Director Joe Dante had just worked with Spielberg on the *Twilight Zone* movie, and *Gremlins* became his biggest hit.

Folk musician Hoyt Axton opens the film as financially insolvent inventor Randall Peltzer. He finds an adorable creature called a mogwai in a Chinatown antiques shop, but the owner will not sell it to him. The owner's grandson sells the mogwai to Randall behind his grandfather's back.

There are three rules for the mogwai: No bright lights, don't get it wet, and don't feed it after midnight.

Randall gives Billy the mogwai and says his name is Gizmo. Comedian Howie Mandel provides the voice of Gizmo.

Corey Feldman appears as Billy's friend Pete, who spills water on Gizmo and triggers the events of the rest of the movie.

When Gizmo gets wet, five new mogwai appear on his back. They trick Billy into feeding them after midnight and they eventually become the evil titular gremlins.

The way the creatures reproduce is similar to how you grow a Chia Pet, a product that had entered the market in 1982.

At this point the film becomes violent because of the gremlins's "kill or be killed" behavior. *Gremlins* was rated PG, released prior to the creation of the PG-13 rating. (Cinematic peer *Sixteen Candles* was also rated PG, despite full female nudity and strong adult language.)

A gremlin named Stripe emerges as the main villain of the movie. He's the only gremlin to survive the initial containment effort and uses a local swimming pool to reproduce en masse.

The gremlins are photophobic—afraid of light—and Stripe is eventually killed by a skylight. Gizmo has remained in his cute mogwai form throughout the movie and is the one who kills Stripe and saves the day.

Eighties "It Girl" Phoebe Cates appears as Billy's girlfriend Kate. She deters the gremlins with a camera flash in order to escape. She also has one of the movie's best-worst lines as she describes how her father died while trapped in a chimney in a Santa Claus costume.

Eventually, the Chinatown shopkeeper arrives and takes Gizmo back.

The idea of gremlins is quite old, with roots in British folklore. They're most closely associated with aircraft—mischief-makers who are responsible for the random things that can go wrong during flights. In fact, a gremlin plays a major role in Steven Spielberg's antecedent 1983 film adaptation *The Twilight Zone* in the segment where an already-panicky airplane passenger sees a gremlin and is taken to be mentally ill. John Lithgow plays the passenger.

Joe Dante's odd knack for funny horror included the heavily self-referential and ironic sense of humor featured in Gremlins. He was creative consultant for the cult children's show Eerie, Indiana. The short-lived show's final episode broke the fourth wall, with Dante appearing as himself as the director.

MIRACLE ON
34TH STREET

Released in 1947, *Miracle on 34th Street* tapped
into the same good feeling created by the
magical realism of 1946's *It's a Wonderful Life*.
But Miracle was made on a much smaller
budget and earned that back several times over.

Maureen O'Hara stars as Doris Walker, a divorced mother who works as an event director at the flagship Macy's in New York. Natalie Wood plays her daughter Susan.

Edmund Gwenn won an Academy Award for his role as Kris Kringle. Kringle notices that the professional Santa for the Macy's Thanksgiving Day Parade is drunk, and he complains to Doris. She's struck by his resemblance to Santa Claus and asks if he'll take the job instead.

Child star Natalie Wood was just 8 when she was cast in Miracle on 34th Street.

Kris Kringle is so successful as the parade's Santa Claus that Doris hires him as the store Santa for the whole Christmas season. He immediately shows that he is a Santa of integrity, pointing shoppers toward better deals at other stores and gaining a loyal following.

The real-life rivalry between Macy's and Gimbels contributes to the plot of *Miracle on 34th Street*. It was so well known in the first half of the 20th century that the expression "Does Macy's tell Gimbels?" stood in for the general idea that competitors don't tip one another off.

Macy's and Gimbels also had competing
Thanksgiving Day parades.

Doris Walker's divorced status made her an
unusual film character—in fact, Maureen O'Hara
was unhappily married at the time and unable to
divorce because of her Irish Catholic faith. Her
first marriage had been annulled when she came
to Hollywood. She eventually did divorce her
second husband.

While Doris is at work, handsome attorney neighbor Fred brings Susan to Macy's to see Santa Claus. Doris is a pragmatist and Susan does not believe in Santa Claus, so Doris asks Kris Kringle to be honest with Susan and tell her he's playing a role—he's already been very candid with customers about other things. But he insists to Susan that he is the real Santa Claus.

Susan sees Kris Kringle speak Dutch to a young girl and it makes her wonder if Santa could be real after all. Doris begins to worry and plans to let Kringle go based on his belief that he is Santa, but she's prevented by the founder of Macy's.

The character R. H. Macy appears in the film, but the real R. H. Macy died in 1877. The Macy family sold the store in 1895.

Kris Kringle's magnanimous approach to Christmastime sales creates a feeling of rivalry among the New York department stores, as they compete to see who can refer away the most business.

In the film, Kris Kringle makes peace between R. H. Macy and "Mr. Gimbel," who is also a fictional character. Gimbels was founded by Adam Gimbel but went public in the 1920s.

The villain of the story is scheming Granville Sawyer, played by typecast heel Porter Hall. Sawyer is upset by the way Kris Kringle treats him during a psychological evaluation. Later, Kringle hits Sawyer with his cane in response to some bad behavior. Sawyer takes a dive, exaggerating his "injury" in order to have Kringle committed.

Fred quits his job and takes Kris Kringle's case, facing off in court against a grinchy district attorney.

Mr. Macy testifies that he believes Kringle is really Santa, although he has business motives in play. Either way, his revenues are real.

Fred's showstopper is to call the district attorney's own son to the stand in order to testify that his father has told him Santa Claus is real.

Susan saves the day when she inadvertently creates a postal technicality that proves Kris Kringle is considered to be Santa Claus in the eyes of the government.

The judge is played by Gene Lockhart, father of *Lassie* star June Lockhart. He also played Bob Cratchit in the 1938 version of *A Christmas Carol*.

John Hughes remade *Miracle on 34th Street* in 1994. The original film was adapted several times for film, television, radio, and stage, but Hughes's theatrical remake is perhaps the best known.

Richard Attenborough stars as Kris Kringle. Before 1993's *Jurassic Park*, Attenborough had stopped acting and remained behind the camera as a filmmaker, most notably for 1982's critically acclaimed and financially successful biopic *Gandhi*. But his role as kind, grandfatherly businessman John Hammond created a new generation of fans.

Mara Wilson appears as Susan in Hughes's remake. She was even younger at the time than Natalie Wood had been. Later, she starred in the film adaptation of Roald Dahl's *Matilda*.

Dylan McDermott plays Bryan, née Fred, the attorney and love interest. McDermott has played many attorneys and law enforcement professionals during his thirty-year career.

Hughes changes the pivotal legal point from a postal to a monetary one: if the government can profess "In God We Trust" on its legal tender, then Santa Claus can also be real.

Macy's did not agree to appear in the film, so events instead take place at "Cole's." The Gimbels analogue, "Shopper's Express," is depicted as less of a rival and more of a corporate predator.

Hughes made *Miracle on 34th Street* in an "off year" between writing *Home Alone 2: Lost in New York* and *Home Alone 3*. The former was also set at Christmastime.